CW01150066

Courting the Muse

BRIGID RAVEN-HART

authorHOUSE

AuthorHouse™
1663 Liberty Drive
Bloomington, IN 47403
www.authorhouse.com
Phone: 833-262-8899

© 2021 Brigid Raven-Hart. All rights reserved.

No part of this book may be reproduced, stored in a retrieval system, or transmitted by any means without the written permission of the author.

Published by AuthorHouse 12/03/2020

ISBN: 978-1-6655-0953-4 (sc)
ISBN: 978-1-6655-0951-0 (hc)
ISBN: 978-1-6655-0952-7 (e)

Library of Congress Control Number: 2020923953

Print information available on the last page.

Any people depicted in stock imagery provided by Getty Images are models, and such images are being used for illustrative purposes only.
Certain stock imagery © Getty Images.

This book is printed on acid-free paper.

Because of the dynamic nature of the Internet, any web addresses or links contained in this book may have changed since publication and may no longer be valid. The views expressed in this work are solely those of the author and do not necessarily reflect the views of the publisher, and the publisher hereby disclaims any responsibility for them.

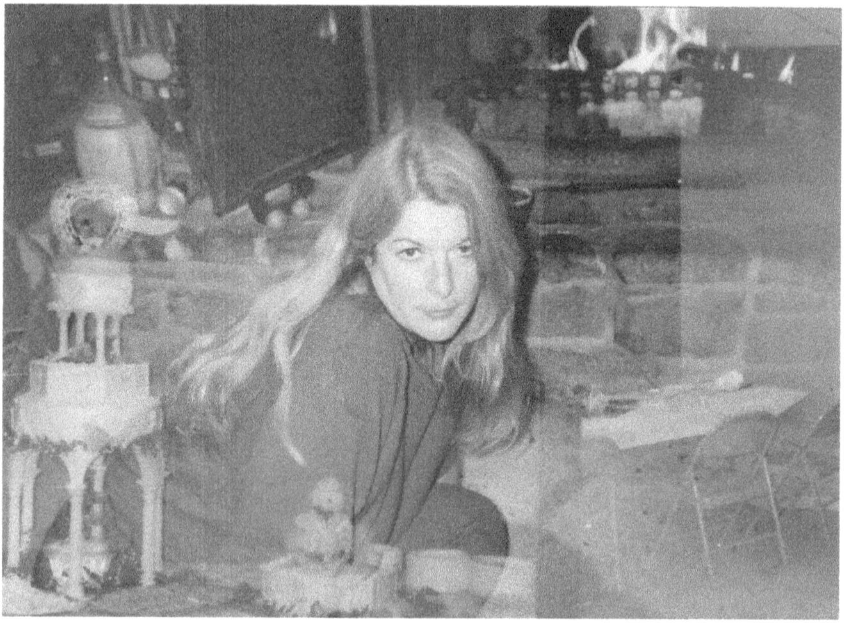

What's in a Name?

In many religions of the world you take a new or additional name at the time of christening, baptism or right of passage. In my faith when you are ready to make a commitment, you chose your own name. One that holds special meaning for you. Often your chosen name has one or more totem animals that embody either traits you feel you possess or traits you are striving to achieve. I pondered my choice of name for many years.

Nothing seemed to be quite right.

My mother's mother, Katherine, always considered me special, out of twenty three wonderful grandchildren, because I was born on her mother's birthday. My Great Gandmother lived her life, raised her family and passed beyond the Vale in Ireland. Neither my mother nor I was privileged to meet her. My mother told me that if she had realized how special that was to her mother she would have named me for my Great Grandmother, Brigid McGrath.

The Raven, though often maligned as a bringer of ill portent, is a fascinating bird possessing intelligence, tenacity and longevity. Much folklore surrounds this totem animal in both Native American practices and Eastern religions, both of which have intrigued me since I was a teenager.

The Hart, a creature of legend and flesh, roams the wildwood never tamed, bowing to no man. Some in earth based and old faith religions, believe the Hart is honored to carry the spirit of the male deity when the God manifests in fleshly form.

Although my faith is commonly thought of as a Goddess based religion it teaches that there must be balance between male and female, the God and the Goddess, for anything of merit and substance to be achieved. We are, after all, two halves of the same whole who nourish and enrich each others inner spirit.

This, then, is how I have come to be Brigid Raven-Hart with my faith rooted in Celtic lore and a strong influence from Native American wisdom and Eastern philosophy.

The following pages contain a collection of verse that have been gifted to me from my Muse over many years. When she graces me with her presence, I've learned, I had better have pen and paper ready. The following pages contain a collection of verse that I hope you will enjoy. Some that will, perhaps, make you smile and some that, I hope, will make you think about our past and our possible future and the choices we make each day.

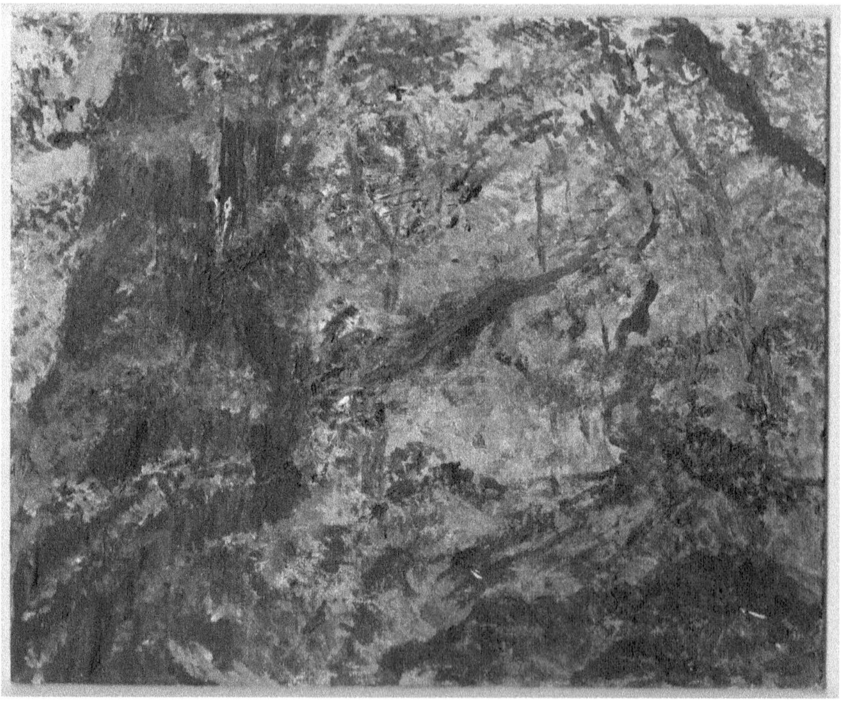

Gift of the Muse

The Muse keeps her ear to the ground

Listening for the Stampede

As it grows nearer and nearer

She knocks loudly on the door of my mind

Open a crack and in she flies

With images that tumble and flash

"Quickly", she urges, "write them all down"

Before they are gone never again to be found

The flood of ideas, questions and thoughts

Makes for a heady brew

No pity has she for my battered brain

As the stampede plunges on through

Perhaps, if I'm lucky, I get half of them down

As they head off for the horizon

No doubt to find some other listening Muse

Who then wakens her very own scribe

I wonder as I read what is written

Where does it all come from

And if we are in there my Muse and I

Or if all of the Muses and personal scribes

Are just part of a ribbon in Time

If she knows she never says

But sometimes it feels like she smiles

From the corner of my eye

Or around the next bend

I await her coming to revel again

As her gift to me, the amazing Stampede

Leaves jewels in my mind from an Otherwhen

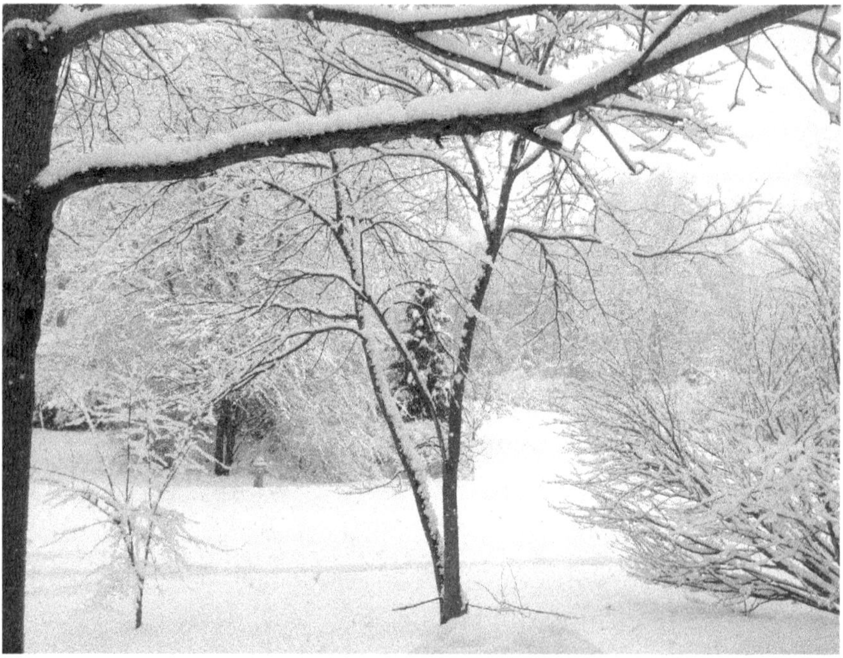

Twas' the month before Christmas and the ad's did abound

Diamonds and sapphires and gas hogs all around

From Wal-mart to Saks, don't forget Andy Mohr

All hawking their great sales, all telling the score

The economy trembles and peeks over the edge

Our 401K simply dribbles away

The gas bill goes higher, the electric bill too

How in the world will a diamond help you?

A friend said he misses the days of his youth racing

down in the morning, to rip open gifts

Nothing more was expected than to rip and to tear,

show up at the table and eat all that was there

This year he is Santa with all that implies and

the Elves are in the unemployment line

Magic Dust costs a fortune so the reindeer's can't fly

Yes this year is different for most everyone
leaner and tighter but just as much fun
More time for your friends and for family bonds,
sharing your munchies, telling stories all around
And as we look back o're the year almost done we
see with amazement what history has won
An impossible happening, a black President was
chosen to rule by the public's consent

Can we dare once again to think about "Hope"?
To drop just a bit of the "Cynical Cloak"
That we've kept wrapped so tightly around all of our thoughts
And focus the fight against the Evil that's been wrought

As we sing all our songs and celebrate "Faith"
no mater "God's" outfit, color or face
Put up our bright trees or burn the Yule Log,
dine on our favorites, pass the egg nog
Let us hold tightly in our hearts, thoughts & prayers the
knowledge that "Difference" is the "Divine Plan"

Since the dawn of time it's the contrasts we see
that take the breath from you and me

If we gather together with "Love" & "Grace" embracing
our differences with "Hope" & "Faith"
Then maybe, just maybe if we work as a team,
respecting each other's different traditions
Helping each other as much as we can to all do
the right thing when choice is at hand
We will learn what "the Divine" always knew, that
the canvas of life contains all of the hues

May you treasure your family, your friends and this
world that we live on together in peace and in peril
May blessings reign down for each good thing you do
from whomever it is you say your prayers to
May your life bring you joy with health and hope and
a future that's wrapped in a Rainbow Cloak
All of these things we wish for you, with harm
to no one from hearts that be true.

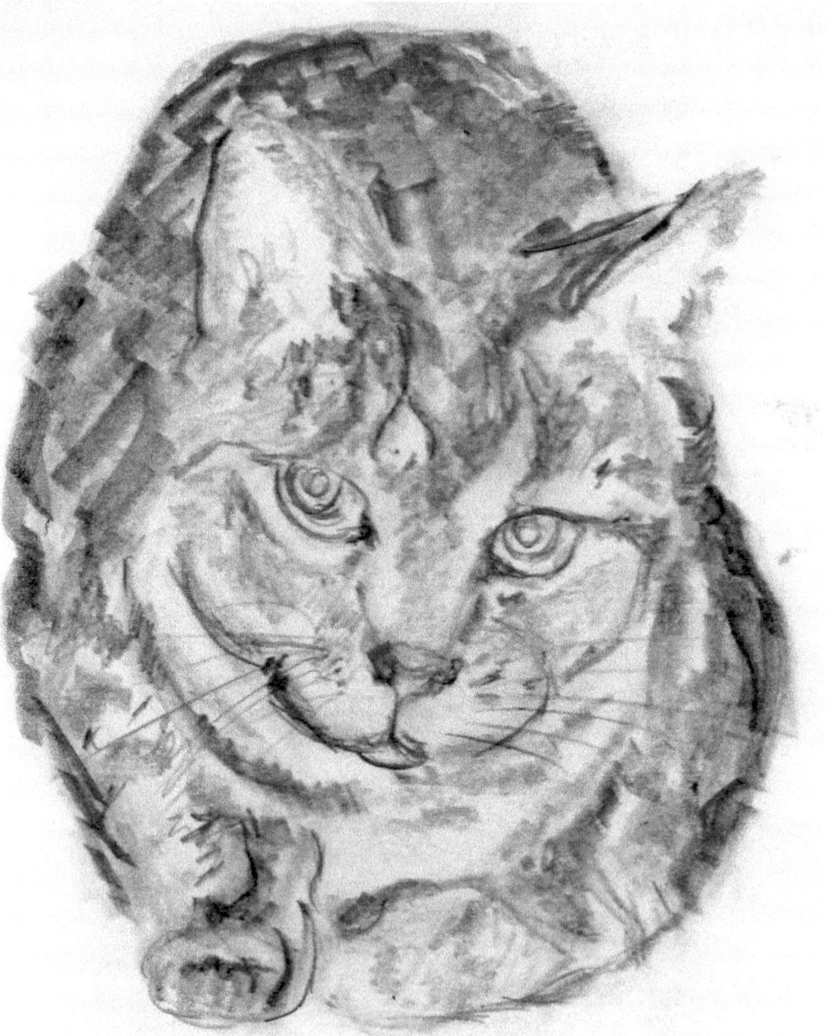

A Good Life

Switchbacks and Slaloms, Challenges and Joys

Life is a heady drug

A gift to be treasured and nurtured and honored

Not for the weak or fainthearted

Be the best You can be in all that you do and say

At your work, at your play, with family and friends

Keep your Music alive and keep sharing

The wonderful gifts you possess

Plan for tomorrow, but Live for Today

So easy to lose sight of that

Some days are like diamonds but some are like mud

Learn the lesson, move on, breathe the Light

Treasure your memories, keep them close to your heart

Without losing yourself in the past

Look to Tomorrow with Love and with kindness

Learn well to Think, Wait and Hope

Be aware and prepared with a positive mind

But never succumb to the "Fear"

It gives no good thing and takes all that you have

Leaving you nothing but broken inside

I am glad for the time I have known you

Proud to count You as a friend

I wish you good things in your future

And thank you for sharing your past

Blessed Be

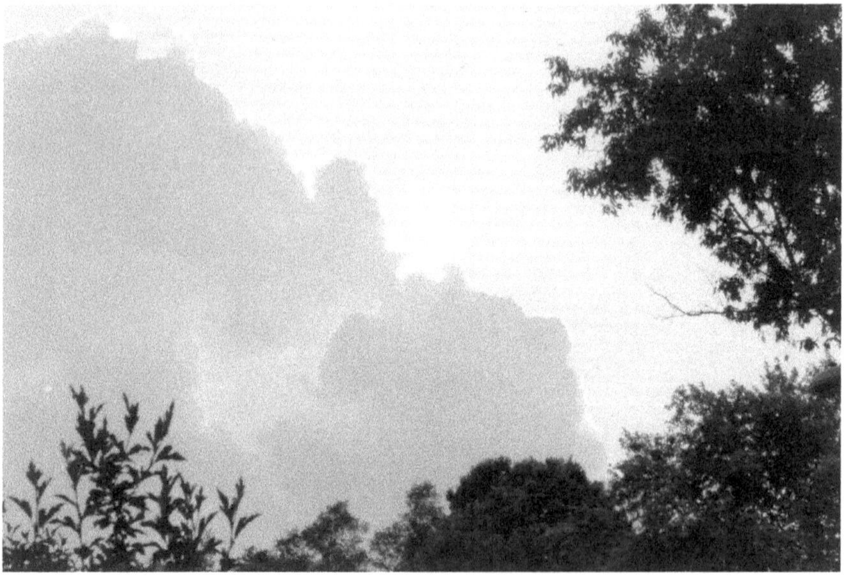

Morning

In the mists of a dawning day

Hidden in the haze

Lives the light that sweeps the mind

Holding cobwebs all at bay

A clarity at first light

Never as clear the rest of the day

But you must wake up and embrace it

Before the message fades away

So breathe deep the mist of the morning

Hold Holy the Song of this Day

Embrace all the truth your heart can bear

And then, be on your way

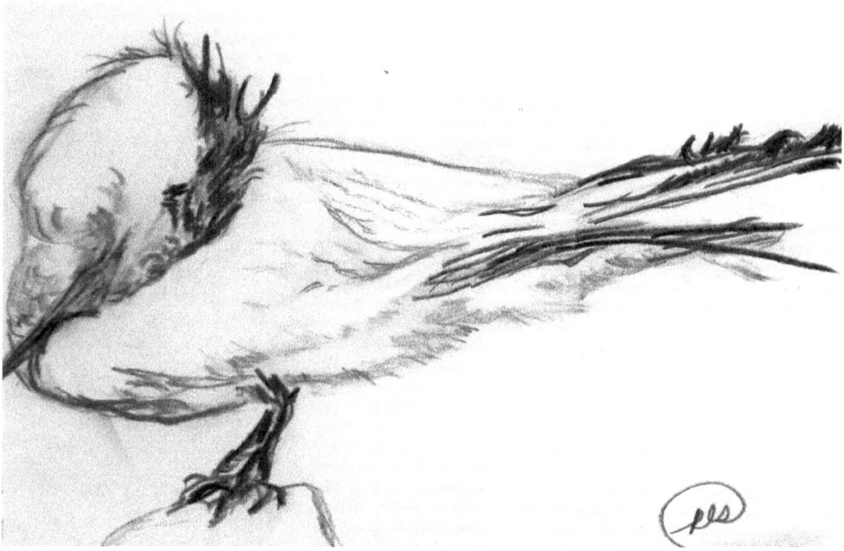

Time

Time is a comfort

Time is a threat

Sometimes a reward

Sometimes a regret

The ticking of a watch

The passing of the sun

The beginning of the day

And when the day is done

The history of mankind

The passing of the days

The time from birth to 18

The time of end of days

The times that come between us

The times that bring us close

The time when fear does rule us

The time I need you most

The time of Birth, the time of Death

The time of Tests and Faith

The time that least becomes us

Is the time of our own Fate

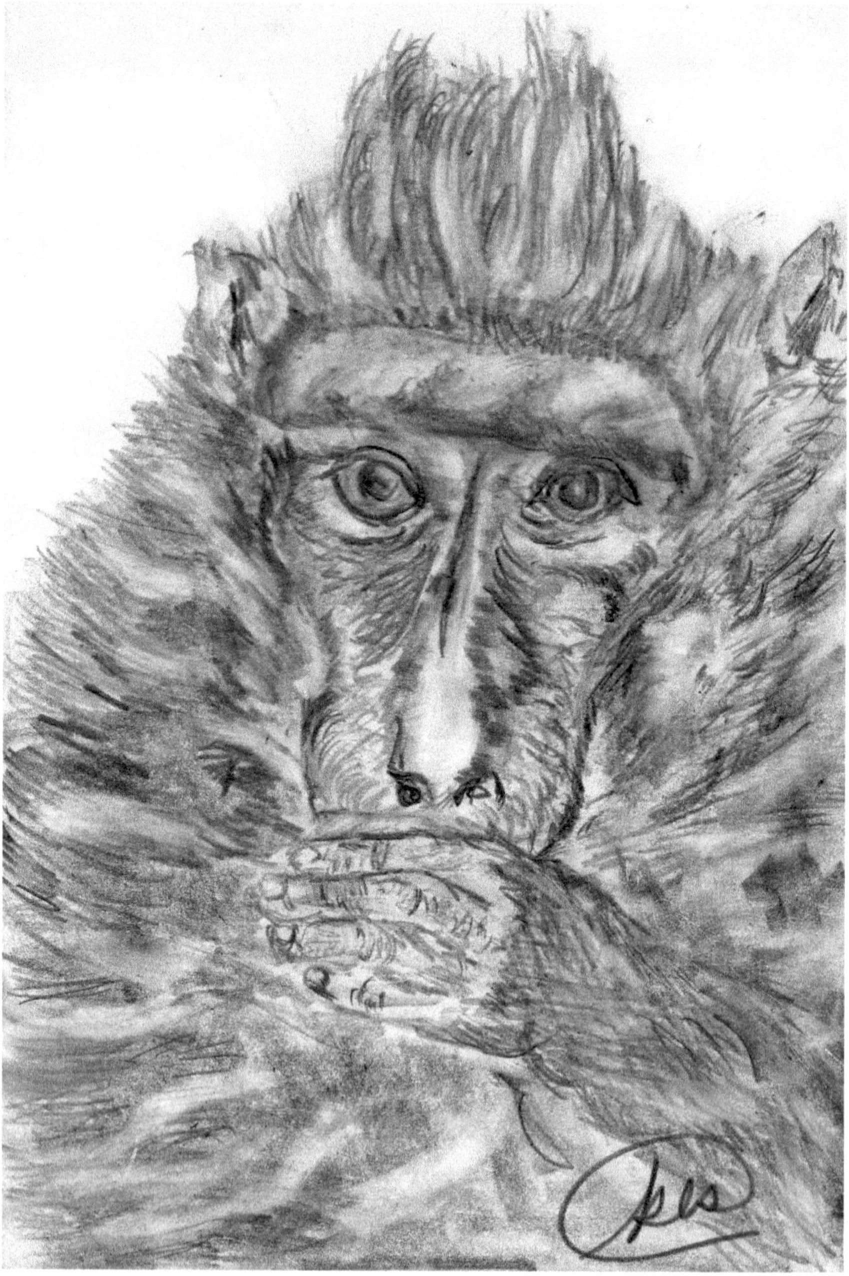

Odd Balls

The richness of life is determined

By the richness of the people in your world

The more complex and eclectic they are

The more real and intense is their story

The greater the intensity of the story

The better chance it has to change the world

So how many odd balls do you know

Who will fight for this our Earth

To save it we need to change it

To save it we all need to care

To matter at all in this continuum

We need to join together and prepare

When the news heralds every morning

Torture and Mayhem abroad

In financial news Greed and Avarice lead

Domestic Violence, Child Abuse, Police Brutality

These are the bullet points on the morning news

What you ingest with your breakfast

Neglected children, strung out youth, broken

soldiers home, but not really

And we call this a civilized society?

My friends it is time to take action

Unless this is your idea of a civilized world.

Distraction and division will not save the day

Unite and fight to find a better way

Embrace all the Odd Balls you're privileged to know

Keep your heart open for new ones each day

Judge not by the outside anyone that your meet

Look deeper to measure their Soul

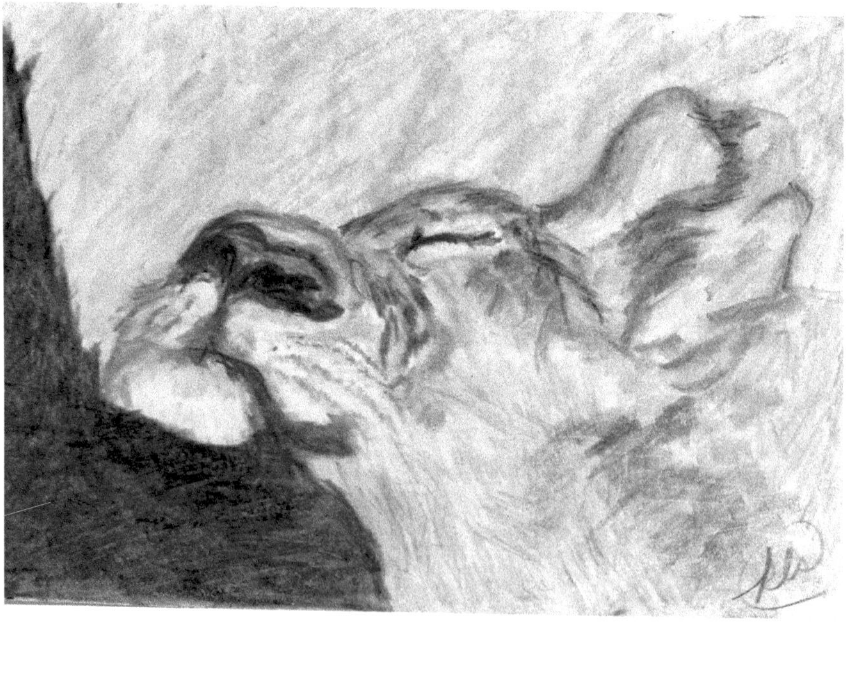

Stuff, Plans and Deeds

"Stuff" is to space, as "Plans" are to time,

Their value can surely be argued

We fill up our home, office and car

Mostly with stuff we need not!

The truth be told, most of that "Stuff"

Never sees the light of the day

When the drawers and doors will open no more

You find yourself moving away

And so it is with "Plans" and "Time"

You keep meaning to lunch with your friends

To meet at the pub, tip a pint, tell a tale

Catch a show with your family, toss the football around.

Go to a party, sit down write a letter

Toss the Frisbee with the dog in the yard

Pick up your e-mail, knit Mom a scarf

Hug your children, pet the cat, plant a garden

But "Deeds" make your life and they rarely meet "Plans"

For people like you and me

Go to work, clean the house, get the groceries

Cook the meals, pay the bills, go to bed, start again

When the circle draws down on this lifetime

Will your "Deeds" have fulfilled your "Plans"

Will you smile to yourself and know life was well met

And be ready to rise up again

Or will you lie in a bed of regrets

With bitterness as your companion

In a room full of stuff you are leaving behind

With the world no better than you found it

Such is the riddle of "Stuff, Plans & Deeds"

I wish you good luck in the solving

A balance there is I am certain of that

I'm just having trouble finding it.

2015

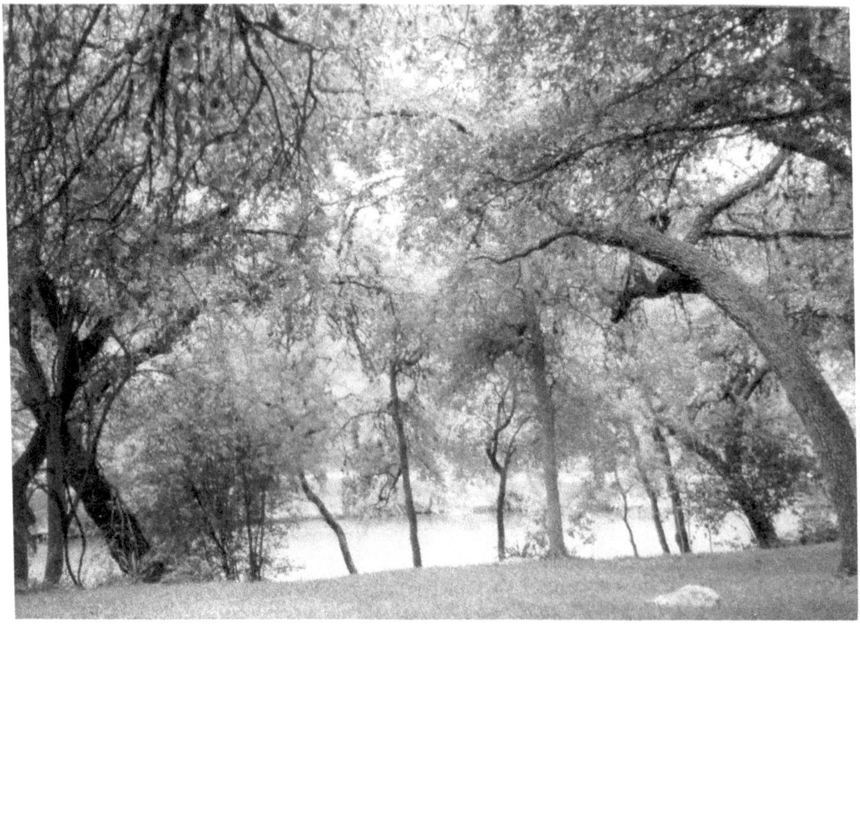

Lessons

Providence my faithful friend

Steer my ship to port

I am weary beyond words

Sick of heart and soul

Serendipity it seems

Comes only after trials

That wring you dry of all you've been

And leave you lost and wild

At least it seems so for a time

But then the mist does clear

And providence though painful

Will teach you lessons bright and dear

Whatever name you go by

Whatever port you're from

I bid welcome this bright day

The future to become

A Maidens Tale

In days of old, when knights were bold

And folks bathed none too often

It was, my friend, pure chivalry

That came to save the day

Fair maiden, laden and distressed

This burden she must bear

Look yonder on that grassy knoll

A knight in armor standing there

Tis only boiled leather that he wears

Yet better than soiled silks

If I can but keep upwind of him

I rather like his ilk

Hark! He comes to rescue me

From my dreary trudging way

"Good morning Lady, may I help"

You see it's on my way

In days of old

When knights were bold

And folks bathed

None too often

1997

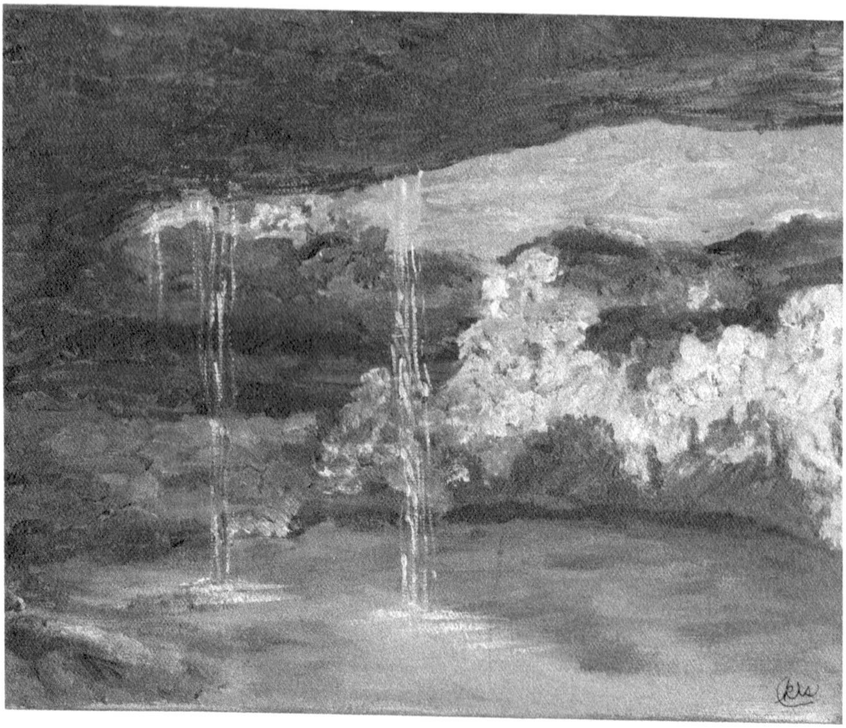

Blessed Be

Blessed Be our planet Earth, without which all would perish

Blessed Be the Forests, Meadows, Plains and Mountains too

Blessed Be the Waters and all who live beneath

Blessed Be the Creatures Wild, living globally

Blessed Be each Sunrise and every day it brings

Blessed Be the Rain and Snow that make the trees and flowers grow

Blessed Be the Sun that warms and feeds the Land

Blessed Be the Sunsets that signal each day's end

Blessed be the Moonrise in all her majesty

Blessed be the Shining Stars from all eternity

Blessed Be the Web of Life in its great symmetry

Blessed Be the Children, of all nationalities

Blessed Be the Aged, who look back upon their memories

Blessed Be the Youth, for they must shape the future

Blessed Be Hard Working Folk who strive to save tomorrow

Blessed Be the Strength of Love, that takes

us through our darkest hours

Blessed Be our Furry Friends who never judge,

never bend, but wag us home each day

Blessed Be the Strength of Friendship to embrace our different customs

Blessed Be Forgiveness when we should go astray

Blessed Be our Partners and our Families every day

Blessed Be the Healers thoughout all humanity

Blessed Be, oh Blessed Be our Rich Diversity

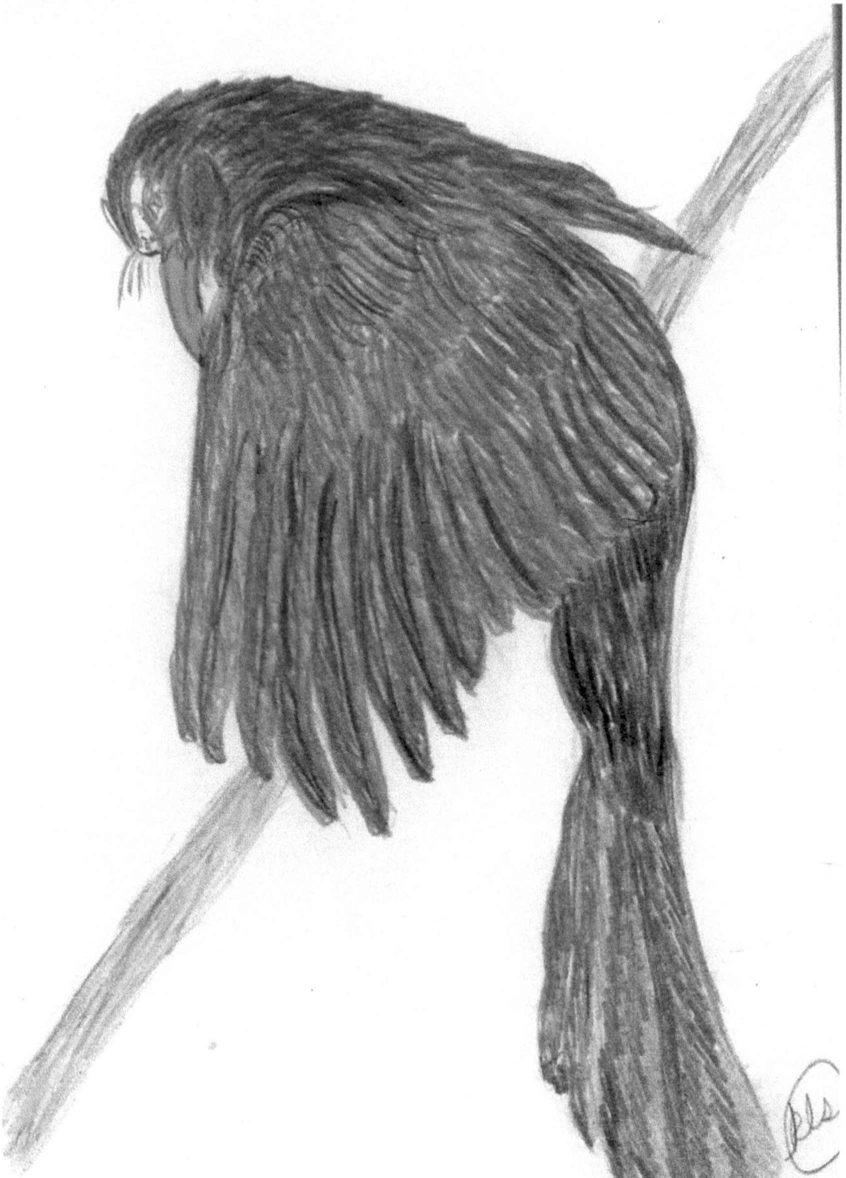

Alone

Sitting on an iceberg
    Floating out in space
        Lonely and abandoned
            Such a stone cold place

No one here to talk to
    No warmth found here at all
        Staring out at nothingness
            No feelings here to call

"Empty" is a place and sound
    No solace here to be found
        No joy, no hope, no warm embrace
            Just a distant "I love you" in its place

12/19

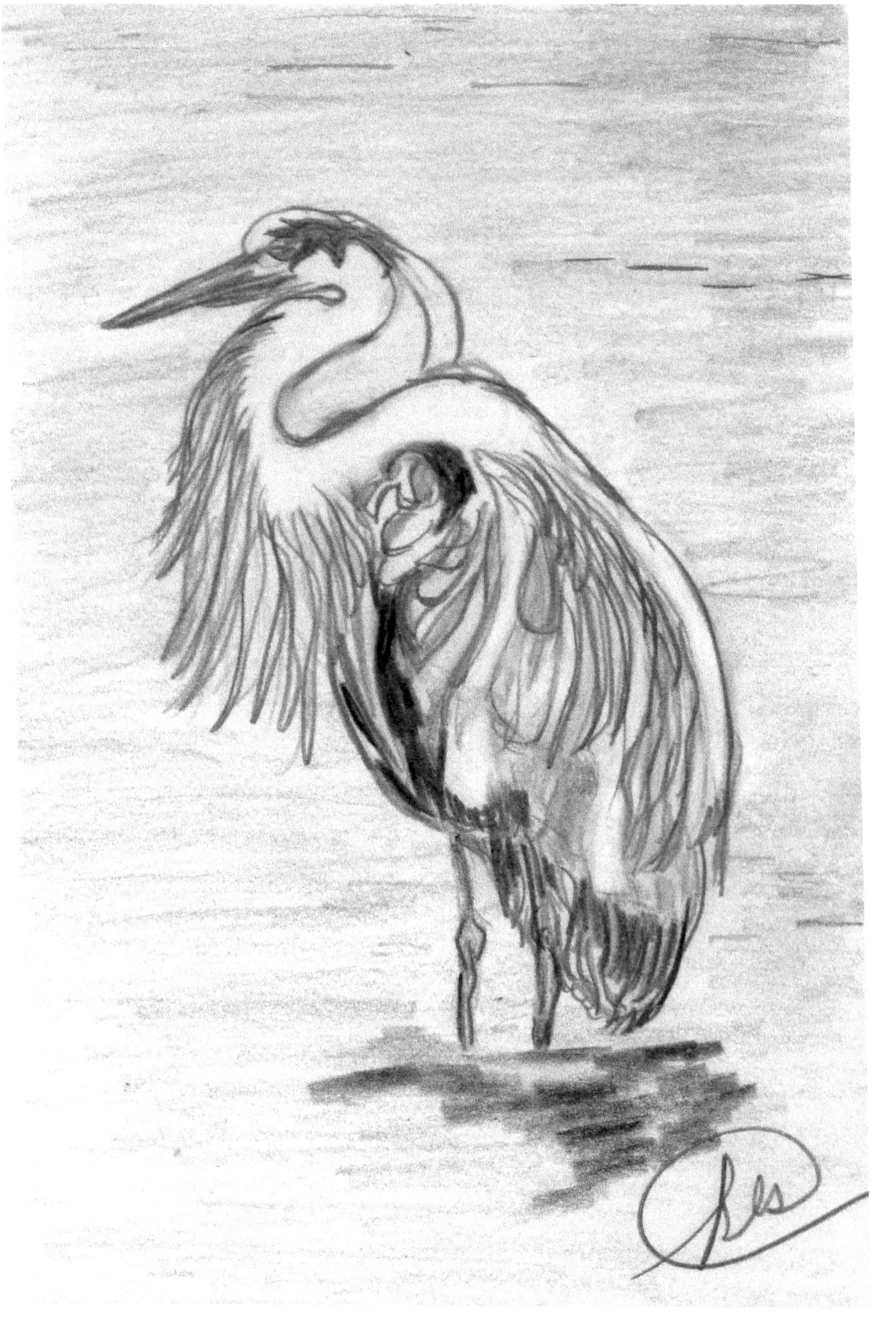

Cleaning House

Attics and basements are my old friends
But not the closets at hallways end
Where fear and anxiety thrive every day
Patrolling the goings of every bi-way

Waking or sleeping on thought filled highways
Looking for secrets and dragons to slay
I can talk to the dead at most any time
It's the living that run me away

These are the doors
That when opened wide
Can lead to your nightmares
And bloody the sky

These are the voyages my soul needs to take
These, the adventures and journeys in time
To dredge up the demons we thought left behind
And vanquish them once and for all

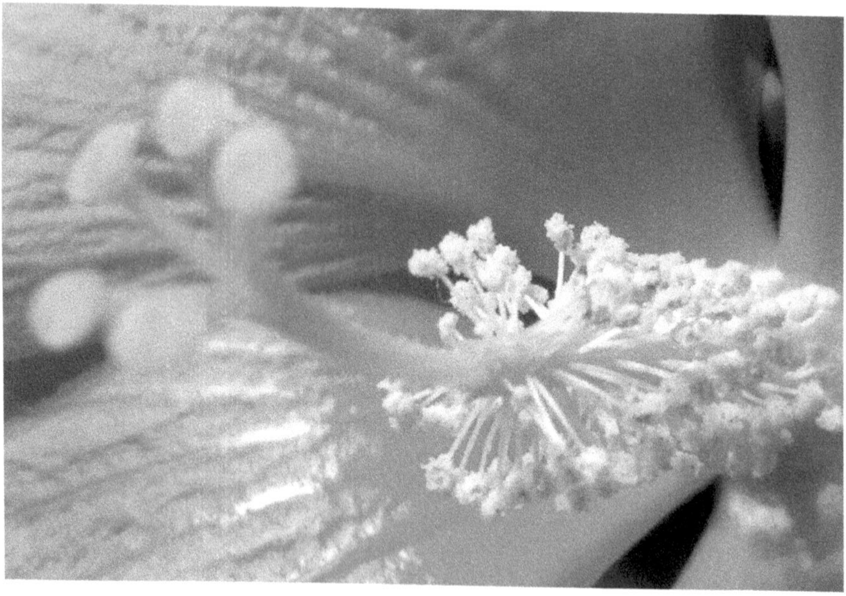

A Song of Thanks

Wrap me in darkness, still all my fears

Wrap me in quiet, to let my wounds heal

Bathe me in starlight, to cleanse my own soul

Share me with moonlight its bright gifts to know

Ensorcelled in bird song do I greet the day

Cloaked in bright sunlight, in mist or in rain

Breathe deep the beauty that swells in the air

All that surrounds me alive and aware

Trees bowing deeply to honor the storm

A hush in the meadow as lightening bursts forth

The rumble of thunder the sound of the rain

The earth to drink deeply, the sun comes again

These powers do free me my soul to take flight

To savor each moment in sun or moon light

As evening approaches I honor this day

And each one before it and all that remain

The chorus of night time swells gentle and sure

The moon swiftly rises its light bright and pure

The stars shining forth in the vault of the sky

The breeze of the evening, the Goddess's sigh

Wrap me in darkness and I'll say goodnight

Wrap me in moonlight my dreams to delight

Wrap me in silence so that I might hear

Her whisper her plan for me into my ear

Goddess Blessings

2005

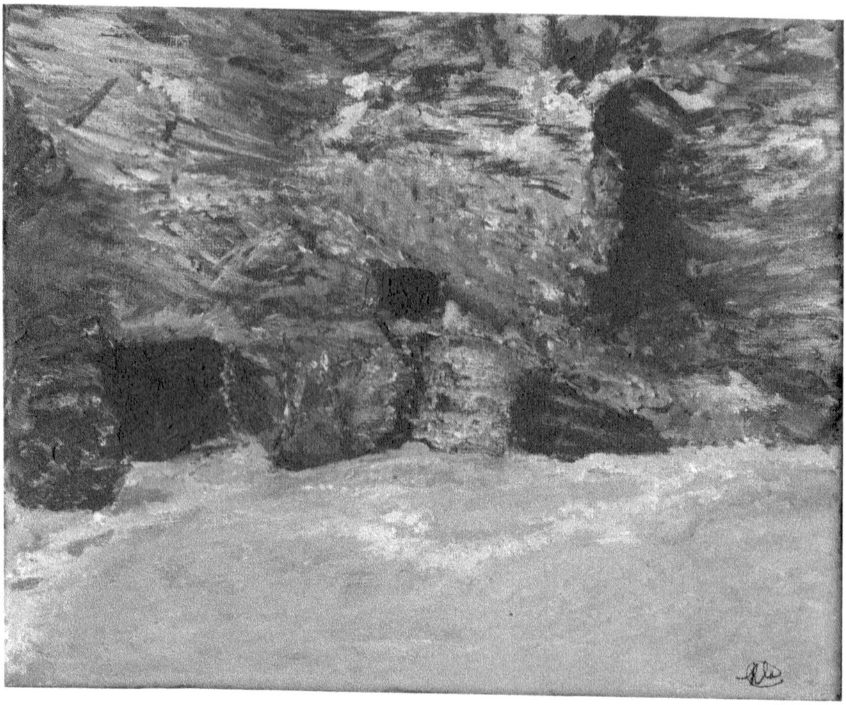

My Old Friend Draconius

Oh where have you gone my friend of old

With breathe of fire and light

Your wit I believe

Is what I miss most

Your interesting turn of mind

Your wisdom has known no equal

Since the dawn of Civilized Man

And Magick! They know nothing of it

One wonders they manage to stand

Yes they think themselves smug, superior

As they blithely destroy Mother Earth

Perhaps you could come and remind them

Of their relative value and worth

Alas! I don't know if they'd listen

Not even to one such as you

An arrogant tribe

Not like to survive

Much beyond Two Thousand and Twenty Two

2002

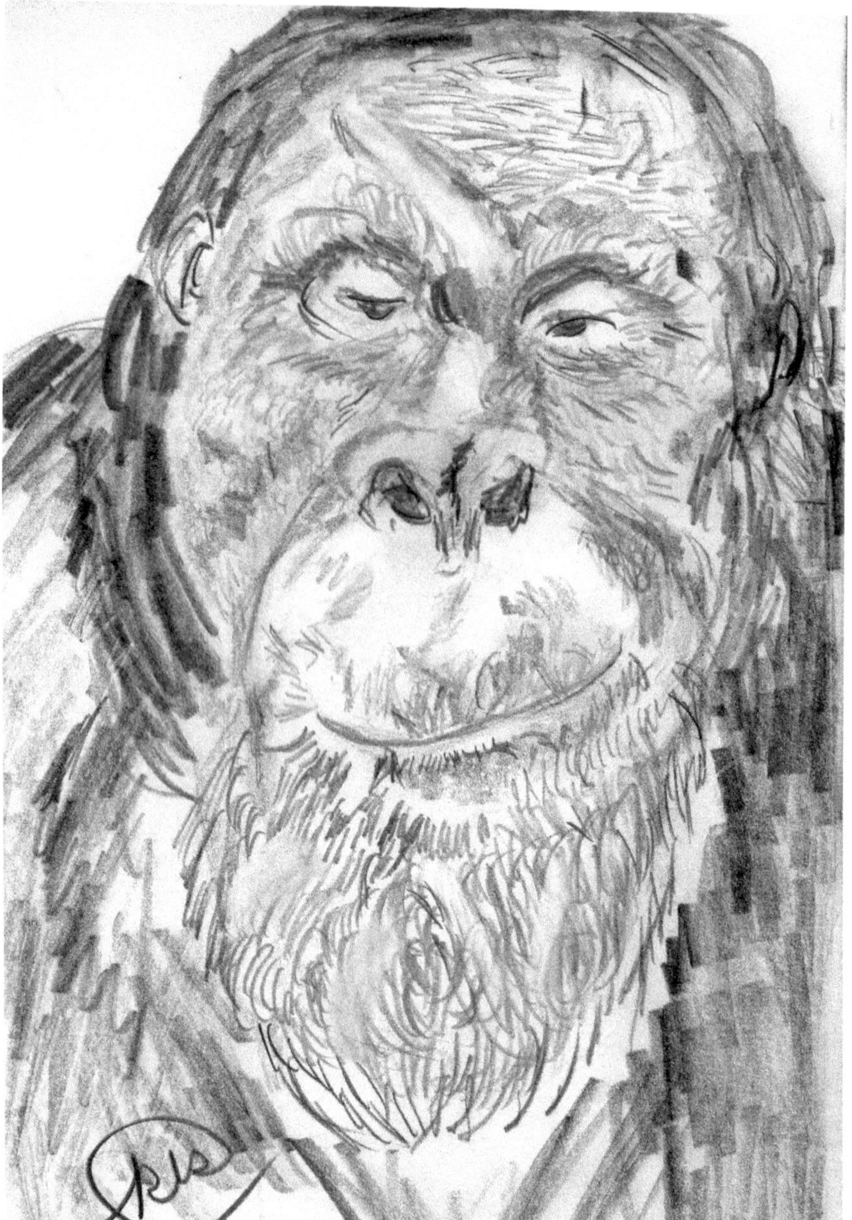

Knowledge

The two edged sword of yesteryear

Is alive and well today

There is no good without evil

And evil shall never hold sway

So where does this paradox leads us

In our quest for truth and might?

Is it a dead end alley?

Should we give up for the night?

Or light our lanterns in the daylight

As the ancient sage proclaimed

To seek someone who spoke truthfully

Without any fear or shame

There is no light without darkness

There is no fear without joy

There is no pain without pleasure

There is no truth without lies

The sword, it would seem, is working quite well

In even this modern age

I'd say there are no easy answers

So let us bring on the new day!

'06

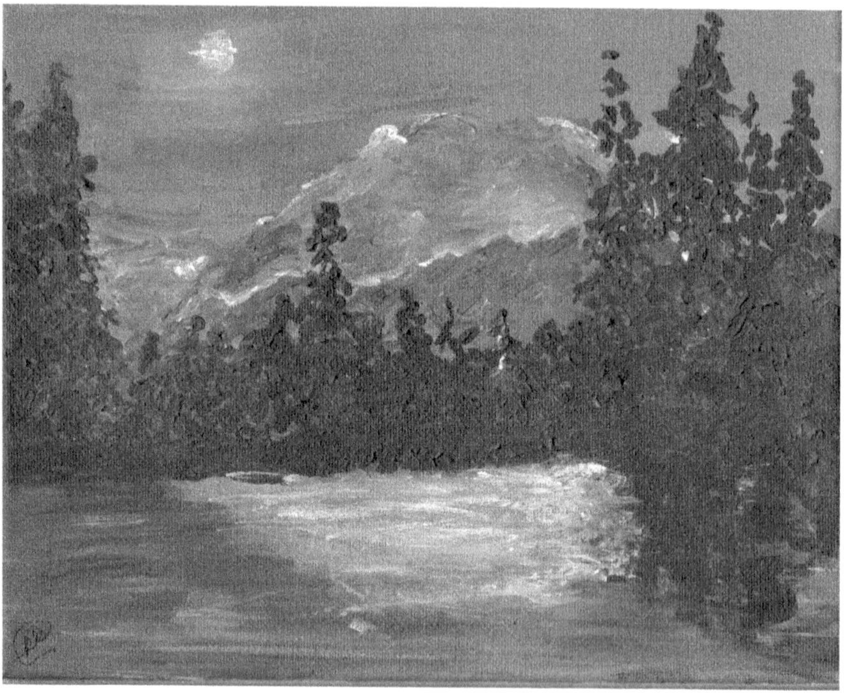

Paradox

Nightfall glides over the mountaintops

Peaceful and serene

Who would guess from the sight below

Our world has no part in this dream

Ours is a place where chaos reigns

Each group absolute and right

Each dogma blessed by this god or that

Each atrocity a holy right

A holy war of godliness

A war of patriotism

Death and sorrow the big winners here

The insane run the institution

How can it be in each generation

These heretics rise to power

We turn a blind eye refusing to see

'Til we've reached the desperate hour

When thousands of people have gone to work

To die between heartbeats one morning

Victim's of a madman's planning

Murdered without warning

How can it be that nobody knew

That no one saw it coming

Oh, but we did for years and years

"And the sheep looked up" as their fate kept coming

The sun will rise over the mountaintops

The birds will sing in the morning

The wolf will suckle her cubs in her den

The river will keep on wandering

And we will make war as we speak of peace

And thousands more will die

With all of them righteously claiming

That god was on their side

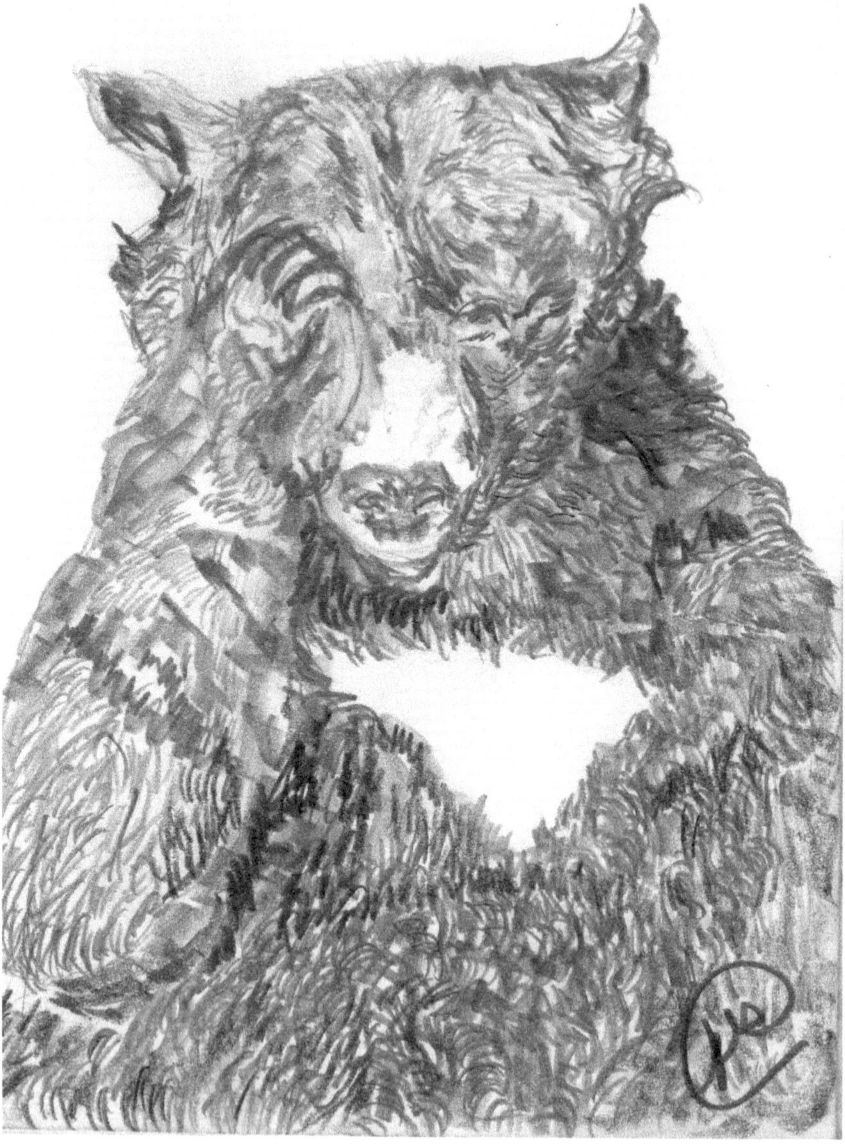

Beneath the Surface

Treading softly through this life
A fragile thing at best
Love and friends and health and freedom
Surely we are blessed

Don't look too hard beneath the surface
Or you might be appalled
At what you see and what you hear
Just walking round the mall

Children angry with their lives
Some even know not why
You say "It's always been this way"
But does that make it right?

Must we constantly repeat

The errors of the past

The same old lies, pathetic tries

Solutions that don't last?

It truly is a wondrous world

But your children know it not

Nor can they believe or even see

What you, most surely, do not

You are the teacher that molds their world

Not the school, not the church or their friends

It's you whom they love and are very proud of

Don't raise them on ashes and venom

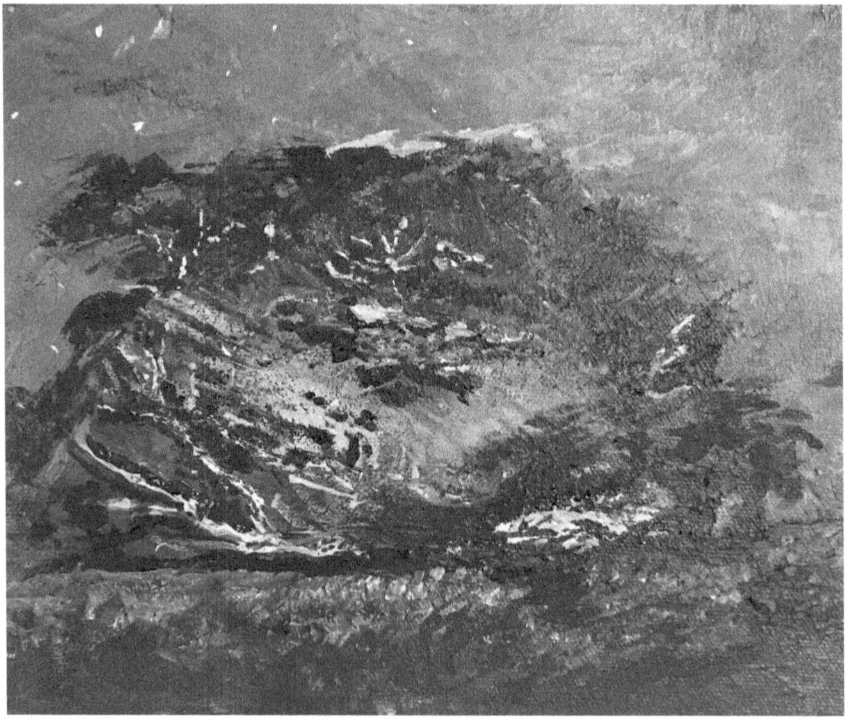

End of Days

In this time of introspection
In this time of Death
In this time of dire illness
In this time of supreme threats

What are we learning about each other
What are we learning of mankind
Some things good and gratifying
Some things foul and horrifying

The government passes a spending bill
To supplement the wellbeing of the people
But Congress recesses to sell their stocks
Before they pass the bill

The President we learn, with little surprise
Is taking the cream from the top
And distributing generously all that he can
To his family, his cronies, himself and himself

Whatever is left will it be divided

Among the working class

Now the government withdraws support of testing

Fearful of learning the truth

The Healers and Helpers give their all

Even up to their own lives

The Teachers teach from remote classrooms

Families spend time together

People re-introduce themselves to Nature

So long have they barred the door

Discovering again the planet they live on

Long walks with family and happy dogs

In the rush and madness

A Truth begins to emerge

We have been fools too busy to notice

That we are all running headlong to Hell

In the supposed seat of Democracy
Sits a liar, a narcissist and a thief
A person who cares nothing for anyone
Delusion his only reality

Even the greediest, most unethical folk
Even those with challenged wits
Even the corrupt politicians
Should never support this president

But sadly somewhere along the way
The "bottom line" became all that mattered
The dog eat dog mentality
Has eroded mankind's gray matter

The "business men" line up at the trough
To get as much of what's left after the presidents grab
To line their pockets greedily
And never pay it back

There are people in our society
Telling workers they can't take precautions
To keep themselves and their families safe
From increased exposure and risk

Wake up America, pay attention
They don't care about you at all
They care about only one thing
How much money they can get their hands on

I hope we survive this time of trials
I hope we learn the hard lessons
I hope we can take back our government
I hope we can save the planet

2019

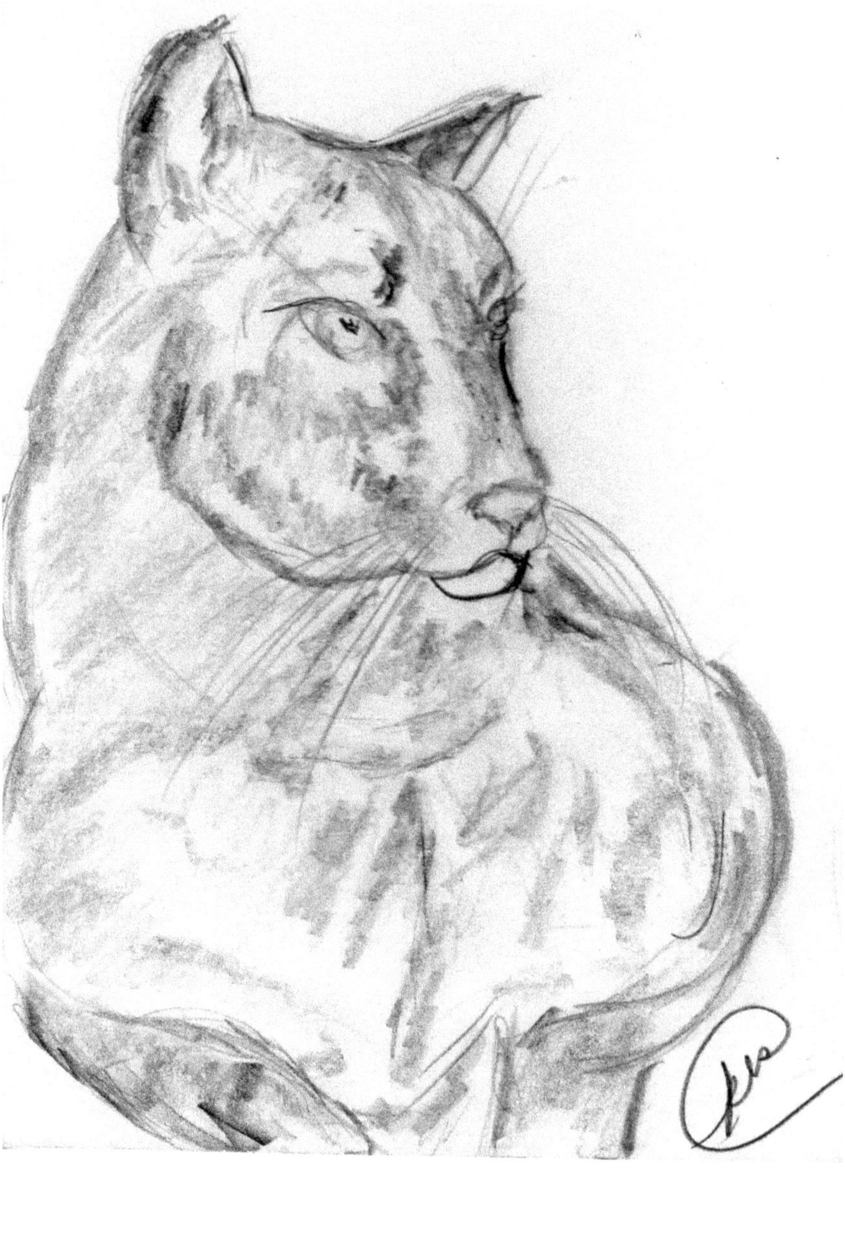

Safe

I'll build me a wall

A wall so high

And no one shall enter

The Kingdom of I

It's lonely in here

With only the sound

Of my own voice

To hear and confound

Oh! The Debates

They are making me mad

Endlessly arguing

This way, then that

No one can hurt you
That's what I first thought
Upon building this fortress
This kingdom I sought

But unbuild the walls?
Can that really be done?
Where will I start?
Where will I run?

Nine summers was I
When I started the wall
I wonder what's out there
And if I shall Fall

02

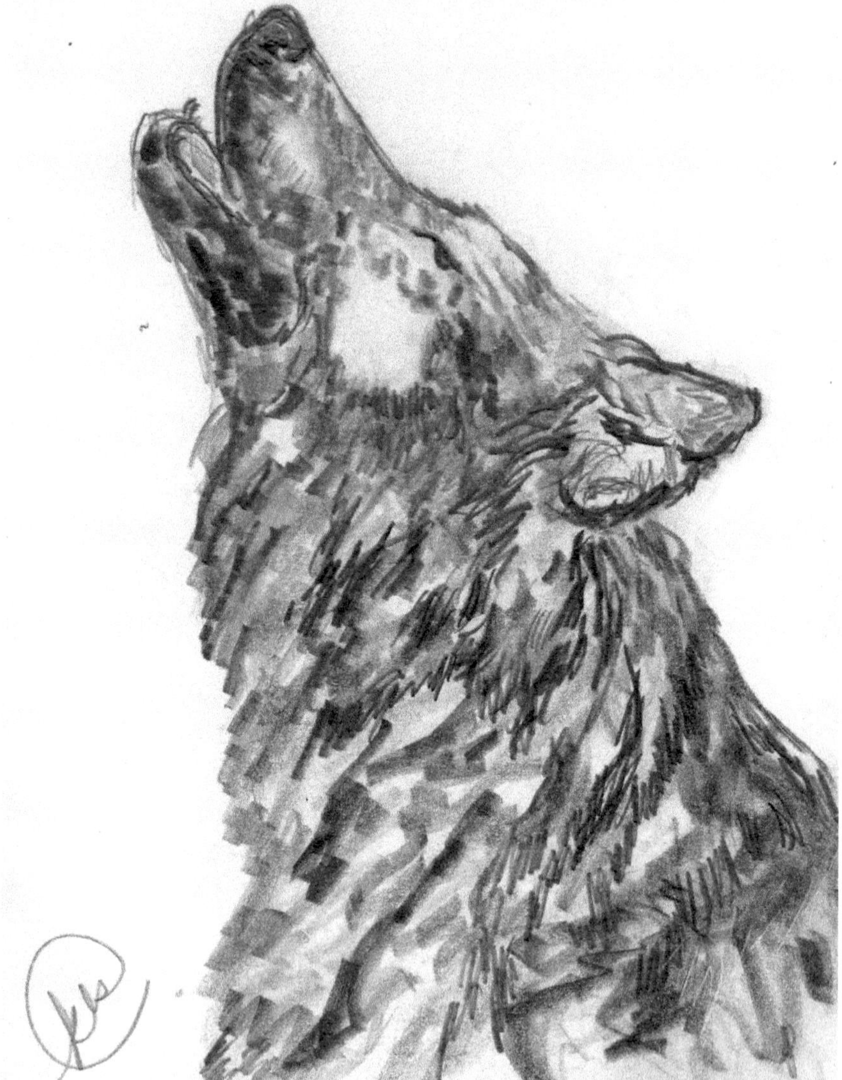

The Well

I go to the well

But the well is dry

I don't know why

I don't know why

I reach into my soul

A reason to find

I cannot cry

I cannot cry

How do we fill the well of Souls

How do we feel again?

How do we save humanity?

From soulless women and men

2017

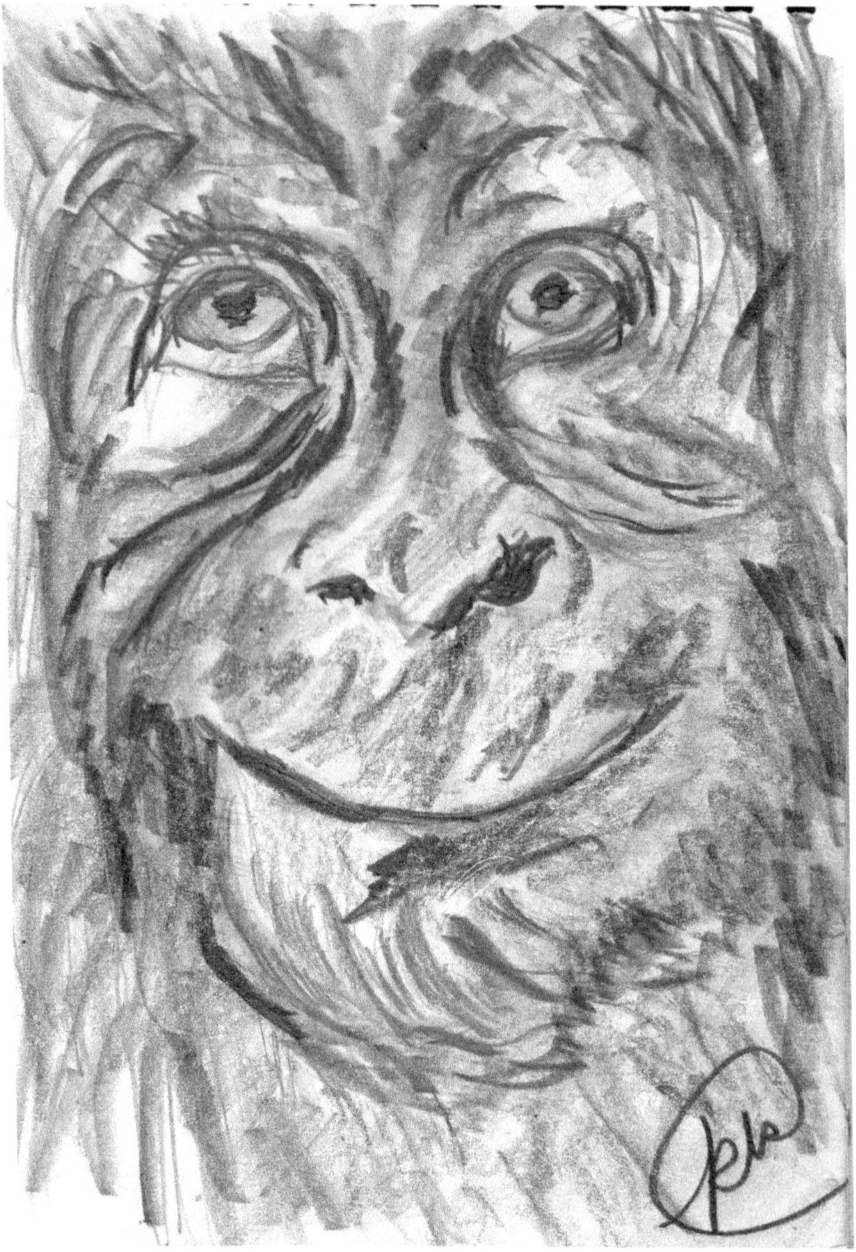

Heroes

So what is a hero?

And rightly you ask

There seem so few these days.

Someone exceptional?

Someone unique?

All of those things

And one thing more.

Ask the man with a Purple Heart

Or a medal pinned to his chest.

"Just staying alive." "Do what you must do."

In point of fact that could be me or you.

What's special about heroes is they're not special at all.

They just hold to their hearts and never let fall

The rules that they live by which set them apart

From the lawless, uncaring and the sick at heart

It's not about money.

It's more about pride.

The clans used to have it,

It was how they survived.

So what happened to change,

In such a drastic way,

The values we give things

Each and every day?

Still I say to you truly, take heart, have no fear.

There are heroes among us, they're really quite near,

Your husband, your neighbor, your wife or your child,

Take a look in your mirror, there is one deep inside.

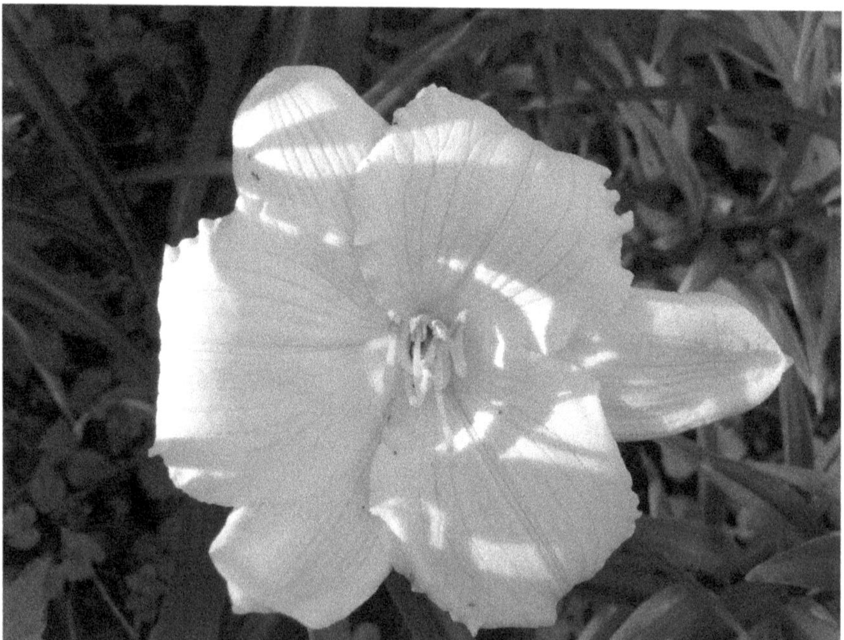

A Prayer for Tomorrow

A garden filled with flowers
each one a work of art
a flash of light bent to the will
of Mother Nature's brush.
A view to take your breath away
your heart to skip a beat
so casually it seems to me
our eyes receive this treat.

And yet there's more the heady smell
of perfume floating high
upon a breeze and through the trees
it brings unbidden sighs.
Yet if we are not careful
we will come to rue the day
we took such things so casually
good sense did not hold sway.

For flowers grow in earth so brown

not in cement and cinders

with so much blood spilled on the ground

the future it will hinder.

The trees can only make the air

we breathe if we are standing

arms uplifted to the skies

roots so firmly planted.

The rain will water all about

if acid is not found

to be it's main ingredient

while carelessness abounds.

The bottom line of dollars and dimes

will very little mean

if the air is gone and the soil is dead

and "Mother" leaves the field.

2004

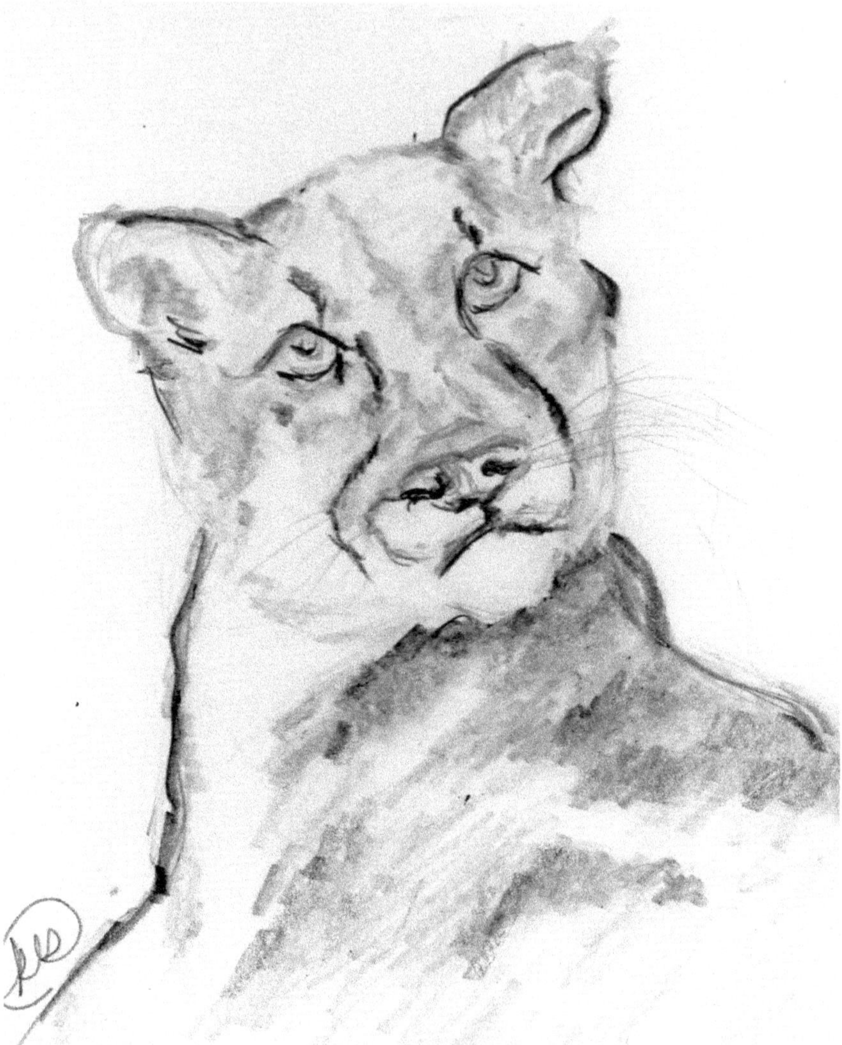

Sweet Balance

Tread softly 'cross the sleeping land
Respect and reverence close at hand
The powers that hold sway here,
Are far beyond our small command.

She is a living breathing soul
This beauty we call "Earth."
All things kept balanced, she sleeps on,
Alas, 'tis not to be.

For we forget ourselves too much
As we ruin all we see
With buildings tall, dams and malls.
We tear down all the trees.

Rape the rain forest, drain the swamps
Poison all the oceans.
Who is it that we think we are,
To take this all for granted?

Beware the sleeping giant
Her patience growing short,
Your arrogance and ignorance
Your own life will abort

Drink deeply the beauty of the land,
Fortune and folly both at hand,
Sing sweetly to her bounteous womb
Her blessings keep you from your tomb.

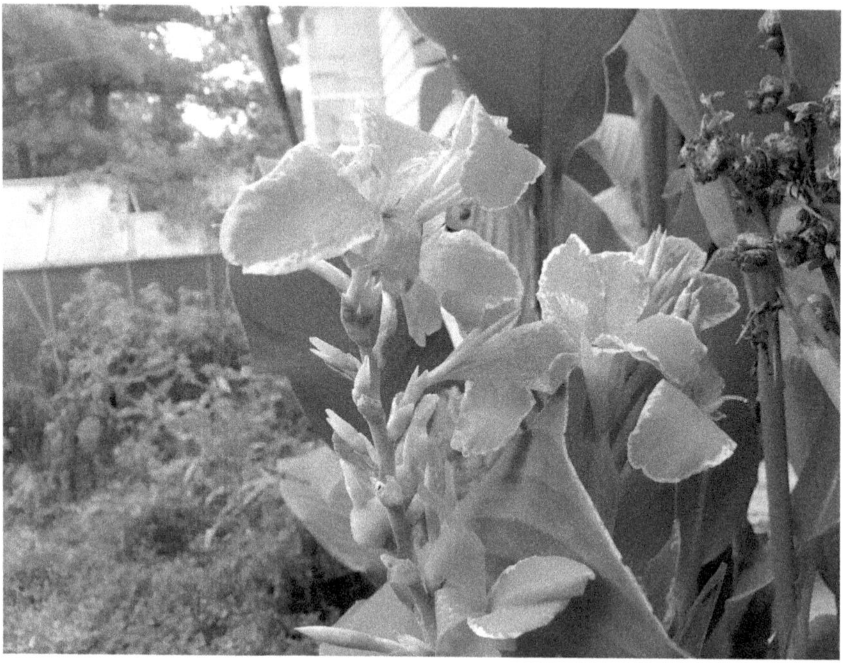

Earth Song

The Earth sings her Song, if only we'd hear

She's been humming this tune for many a year

Harmony, discord, the banging of drums

A warning, a pleading of change that's to come

She's been singing this song for a hundred long years

But we weren't all listening, so we didn't all hear

Some have made changes and those changes help

But so many just turned a deaf ear

Belching their poisons into the air

Spewing their waste never hearing "Beware"

In rivers and streams and oceans alike

Fouled the earth 'neath our feet so it can't support life

The warnings were sounded in the Dustbowl's winds

Again as the Sea storms the Land and moves in

And again as Earth cracks with no green thing in sight

Yet again when the mountains rage fire through the nights

We've reached another Tipping Point

As in the Glaciers melt and weather storms

Things will never again be just as they were

And we - may or may not survive

Much we can do to help our Earth's healing

Of all of the wounds we've inflicted on her

But we must Listen with all of our being

And set our feet on the Path of Healing

Greed has no part in this great endeavor

Great change is the only solution

With or without Mankind doing our part

Mother Earth will perform her Cleansing Ablutions

The author grew up in a small rural town in New Jersey when generational families still happened in this country. Her grandparents were from Lithuania on one side and Ireland on the other. Childhood was filled with chores and responsibilities but also with time when the imagination could travel anywhere it wished to go. Her childhood also contained more time around adults than with other children. This was still the age when children were seen, not heard. She watched and listened and collected pieces of the puzzle of Life.

Her Father wrote poetry, her mother was an artist. Books of all kinds and music were always part of life. Her grandparents were farmers, so the power of Nature was never taken for granted. Throughout this journey, so far, she has experienced a rich variety of people, adventures, cultures, spiritual beliefs and points of view. This added more pieces to that puzzle.

In her twenties the puzzle pieces started to sort themselves out and then the poems started. The pieces are still assembling, they are still sorting and the poems are still coming. This collection of poems could be about anyone.

There are no degrees from schools of higher learning. There are, however, the recommendations of friends and family who have read and related to the poems herein. They are about joy and sorrow, hope and fear, but through it all, they are about people and this amazing Earth that everyone must share and care for.

They are for you.

Lightning Source UK Ltd.
Milton Keynes UK
UKHW011921270223
417761UK00012B/590/J